TABLE O

MW01244917

INTRODUCTION

My name is Jermale Zardies and I'm a convicted felon who was housed in the Louisiana Department of Corrections at the Louisiana State Penitentiary. I'm from New Orleans, Louisiana the home of the French Quarters, Mardi Gras, and great people. I'm forty-one years of age and I graduated from John F. Kennedy High School in New Orleans. I also attended three months of college at Mary Holmes Community College in Westpoint, Mississippi on a basketball scholarship. My parents are the late Mr. Melvin Zardies Jr. and Mrs. Cheryl Zardies, who gave birth to me on January 4, 1975. I have two sisters Mrs. Tamara Andrews, (married to Aaron Andrews) who is the second oldest at 30 and Kierra Oxley, who is the youngest at 24. Kierra has a different father from me and Tamara, who is another father figure in my life, Mr. Frank Oxley. We were well raised children in our younger days, especially having both parents. Well me and my sister managed to have the joy of our parents until tragedy struck on February 4, 1988. Our father suffered from depression after coming home from the United States Marine Corps and unfortunately, it got the best of him. He committed suicide that night and left behind a family that was riddled with deep wounds and scars. Don't give me wrong, we made suffering within look happy. If you were on the outside looking in, you would have never known how we suffered from that event. We loved that man with everything in us for being the husband, father and God-fearing man he was and many others can account for his actions. He was loved by all! As for me I suppressed my feelings for years by trying to overpower them with extracurricular activities, drugs and street life. I first tried marijuana at 15 which was two years after my father's death. I tried it to be cool I guess. Almost every other teenager and family member was doing it and I chose to join the crowd. This lead to me selling it and I went on to the more powerful drugs after, both selling and using them. I became an intense heroin user and I was addicted to not only the drug but the criminal lifestyle that came with it. This lead me to arrest after arrest and having to accept conviction after conviction of my crimes. I ended my misery while being arrested for armed robbery but they lessened my charge to theft because it was a botch scheme that went bad. I was sentenced to 10 years but with the completion of the Re-Entry Program in Angola (L.S.P.), I could serve up to 2 years by receiving a trade and recidivism. I could attain what was required of me by graduating a Welding course and all other classes that was presented before me. I used my time wisely and better myself to become a productive citizen of society by focusing on my sobriety and Spirituality. Me surrendering my life to God (Yahweh) and accepting Jesus Christ (Yahushua) as my Lord and Savior, saved me and turn my inner man away from being manipulated and easily persuaded by Satan. Now I can hear God communicate with me through the righteous choices I make, Scripture and other's godly wisdom. I've found my identity as a man, putting closure to a chapter in my life, in which I thought I controlled. So today I'm free. Free from not knowing where to rest in faith, free from trying to understand the things I've done and do and free from the devil's deception which lead me to unwanted situations and circumstances like prison. Now I look back at my bad choices as lessons to motivate myself. I choose to never travel that negative route again. I will keep trusting in God, knowing Jesus and being obedient to His Word. This is sweet freedom! Freedom, the joy of experiencing unconditional love for self to accept God's purpose in your life. It reveals your identity, gives you closure to negativity and a sincere Spirituality, which helped me turn from a point to where the odds were against me. Remember, anything that doesn't kill you can only make you better. My freedom has rung! Can you hear me now?

I also would like to encourage any person out there that believe in how their story can inspire or motivate others to write a book and self-publish it. You too have a book in you. Look at it as your testimony. One of our responsibilities while we are here on earth is to save other souls and you just never know who life you can touch with your story. You can even save lives. So, stop doubting your capability and start believing in yourself and in what God can do for you. Pick up the pen and start writing! Every one of us has a book in us! I love you all and God bless you guys!

LIVING IN A POETIC SPIRIT

Why Poetry?

Poetry gives one a chance to listen to what's in the inside of people and most of the time you'll find out that you are not the only one thinking or feeling a certain way. It's a voice of correction, direction, and discipline to humanity. Think about it, when someone writes poetry, most of the time it's directed to enlighten, inspire, and motivate the audience. Very seldom have you heard a poem used for negative reasons. Therefore, I chose to focus on poetry and writing stories through it. It's amazing how one feels after reading an inspirational poem that shifts the atmosphere from negative to positive. I possess a passion or rather a purpose to uplift others through my writings. Poetry is an energetic force of compassion that paints the perfect picture of your ideas. It's those inward feelings that some people can't express through openly speaking. A person doesn't always get say what they need to say, but they can write it. For some reason, this stands out to me. Poetry also provides a therapeutic approach to the writer and reader by prescribing a medicine for literature lovers. There's knowledge, wisdom, and understanding included from verse to verse, especially when God's word is presented. It's rehabilitation for the person who needs it, counseling for the listening ear, and most of all freedom. Who wants a life without the silent communication of poetry? It's directed or rather intended to please your quest for answers to you. You are your spirit that dwells in the depth of your being. Everyone needs answers and you can seek them through the lines of truth, trust, and integrity. These credentials lie in the secret spheres that an honest poem of truthfulness withhold. I choose to let it out. I can't withhold what God has stored in me any longer. I feel as if I'm failing Him for not letting this treasure of partiality reign through my passion. A predilection of love and of what God needs us to do. This is why poetry chose me because it knows I can deliver a message through my stories. I took an oath to her, that I will uphold. A marriage that I must be faithful to by protecting her image. To have and to hold until death do us part. I do!

LIVING IN A POETIC SPIRIT

Why does poetry matter to me?

Poetry is another form of expressing yourself or communicating, without opening your mouth to speak. Well, with the exception of open mic poetry, music, and hymns. It's a form of independent freedom that reflects everyday living, feelings, thoughts, and truths to someone who needs to hear or read what you wrote. I first fell in unconditional love with the art while incarcerated in Louisiana State Penitentiary, located in Angola, Louisiana. It was nothing but a supernatural power that helped me discover my talent or rather gift. I grew interested in reading to feed my mind with the richness, knowledge, and serenity in the power of a book. As I read more my mind became a sponge and soaked information into it, that processed a change of my thoughts. I started jotting down data that I thought was important to me and a desire to write what I thought was a need to be heard by other individuals, grew passionately inside of me. While in the Re-Entry Program we had, what was called a morning motivational meeting, to inspire each other through our daily procedures of classes and learning trades. The program had mentors who were selected by the warden himself that had life sentences but chose to change their lives by the grace of God. I was selected to perform the word of the day, in which I not only gave a word, I wrote a poem called "A Woman's Worth" that drew recognition from almost every single person who attended the meeting. I was congratulated and told by many others of how my writing touched them. I understood then, this was a sign of how God will use me. From then, I wrote another poem called "Jesus Walks", that appeared in the Angolite, which is a magazine that publishes inmates writing and articles. This is why poems matter so much to me. Not only do they inspire others but they tell my story. God has a calling on my life because I'm actually still alive today. I've weathered some storms that's unimaginable to some people, but I'm here today to tell my story.

This is writings for all walks of life. No matter what you've been through, there's

something you can relate to in this book. Whether it be work, love, hate, relationships, spirituality, reality, street life, morality, etc. The list goes on. But most of all, there's God's presence through Scripture and facts that He sent Himself, by the means of the Bible and His Spirit. I'm a native of New Orleans, Louisiana who lived a life, being on both sides of God's Law. But I must say my focus is no longer on my past because I'm lead by the Spirit to present it honestly to people. My intentions are to help change someone from a course of destruction, especially the youth because they are our future. I must save a soul like somebody saved mine. Don't misunderstand me, I'm far from perfect, but I'm a 100% better of a person than I was and I need the reader to do the same. All this pertains to poetry because we all have a story to tell. One just must build the courage up to tell it. Poetry chose me because I never had a desire to write period, as a matter of fact, I hated English in high school and writing did not attract my attention. It's when I found that peace and serenity through writing that I let it take control. Now I write on things I never thought in a million years I'll elaborate on. Poetry is my therapy of guidance. It's overall, the best thing that happened to me since accepting Christ and this could be you too. I encourage all to write about their experiences, spiritual awakenings, and paths to become a better person. There's a person in need of your story. I can honestly say I love you all today and I hope and pray you enjoy my story.

HISTORY OF POETRY

The history of poetry is as long as the history of modern man. This explains why ancient Greeks were fond of relaying historical events in the form of poetry. Homer's Odyssey and Iliad being the most well-known examples. Epic poems were the way to transfer your great story to the masses. Many of them took on a rhythmic structure approaching a form of music. That's why most notably hymns were written to be sung. This branch of poetry sprung from the more pleasant side of religion as worshipers looked to exalt their God or gods in song. Not all poetry is rhythmic though. Poetry in prose is poetry written almost as a novel. Individuals used grammatical structure and natural flow of speech rather than rhythmic structure. Some debate that prose poetry is actually poetry though. Many argue that it's focus on narrative and objective truths negate it from being true poetry. While others argue that because of the use of metaphors and heightened attention to language, make it real. There is yet another group who believe it's subversive nature does not fit into either genre. Oscar Wilde picked up prose poetry simply for its subversive nature. Poetry critics are not about to let up on the debate either. The Deluge tablet, carved in stone, of the Gilgamesh epic in Akkadian, circa 2nd millennium BC, is one of the earliest forms. It was believed to be a way of remembering oral history, genealogy, and law. Some Poetry also reflected on fiction. The oldest surviving speculative fiction poem is the "Tale of the Shipwrecked Sailor," written in Hieratic and ascribed a date around 2500 B.C.E. Black poetry refers to poems written by African Americans in the United States of America. It is a subsection of African American literature filled with cadence, intentional repletion and alliteration. African American poetry predates the written word and is linked to a rich oral tradition. Black poetry draws its inspiration from musical traditions such as gospel, blues, jazz and rap. Black poems are inextricably linked to the experience of African Americans through their history in America, from slavery to segregation and the equal rights movement. African American poets as early as the American Revolution wrote verse reflective of the time in which they lived.

The earliest known black American poets: Jupiter Hammon (1711-1800), Lucy Terry (1730-1821) and Phillis Wheatley (1753-1784) constructed their poems on contemporary models. Lucy Terry wrote a brief narrative poem describing an Indian raid, a poem important not so much for its esthetics as for its historical importance. The poem "Bar Fight", was written in 1746 or thereabouts and not published until 1855, is the first poem known to have been written by a black poet. Then came others such as Mya Angelou, Langston Hughes, Tupac Shakur, Alice Walker, Nikki Giovanni and the list goes on and on. I'm truly thankful for the great poetry writers before me because without them this wouldn't be possible. Their writings inspire us to move forward in life to be a better person. I'll forever respect their struggles and history because without them going through what they went through, we wouldn't be where we are today.

GOALS AND EXPECTATIONS

First, my aim is to soothe the reader by comforting them from worldly distractions because at the end of the day, our main purpose here on earth is Afterlife. God communicates to us in ways that some of us may never quite fathom. We as a people need to be open minded to how God speaks to us. All I know and understand is that He does it in a variety of ways. We just must be Wise enough to pay attention. This is for the person who is going through adversity, through struggles, and the pain that life may bring upon. It's also for the one who is established but may need to hear something from another person to humble them. So, as you can see, this is dedicated to all walks of life. I've traveled a road that only God could've stirred my path to freedom. I was stuck in spiritual, mental, emotional, and physical prison. Possessed by demons and evil spirits that we may take for granted as believers. My heart, mind, and outlook on life was manipulated by a dark force that blurred my vision. Drugs, alcohol, and street life was my focus. Honestly, nothing else mattered. Could you imagine being stuck in a state like that? Well that was my past. But there is someone to call on for help and His name is Jesus. He helped me change my way of thinking, which gave me hope. My mind was renewed and my heart felt a godly presence inside it. I was Awaken by His love. It aided in me forgiving myself and others and gave me the courage to ask for others forgiveness. Something I know that would not have taken place on its own. I accepted Jesus as my Lord and Savior and I'm presently looking for a church home to join. My life has changed but it did not get easier because now all the responsibilities, realities, and decisions are to be faced and accounted for. It's been a long and hard journey but the power that's inside me now, will never let me quit. Thanks be to God! My love for self and others are supernaturally and divine because I understand that unconditional love is putting others before self. That was expressed through the greatest act of love ever, when Jesus gave His life for ours. So, I believe in doing His work down here on earth and it's through my gift of writing. I want to inspire someone to do the same. We have souls to save.

We must understand that through being obedient to God, it's a responsibility to reach out to others. My goal is to leave a spiritual legacy for people to follow. To lead like Jesus did. I want to talk to the youth at schools, centers, and prisons. We need more people to reach out to them because of the violence and failure to uplift them. We are part of the problem but we are also the solution being routed by Christ's word. I plan to promote poetry as another form of expression for people still to this day because it can be look upon as an outlet, like Rap, R&B, and other forms of music. Instead of resulting to violence and crime, people can write what they feel to solve confrontation but with some positive individuals at hand to assist.

CHAPTER 1: PHYSICAL POETRY

FATHER GOD HELP ME CHANGE MY WAYS

Ecclesiastes 3:1 There is a time for everything, and a season for every activity under the heavens:

If I am to stand as the man God created me to be

There are some things I must fix about self

Because God's plan is for me is to be righteous and free

No matter what I encounter He's there with help

But sometimes my actions are like I'm fighting his will

With the backsliding and falling victim to Hades

Lord I pray for your guidance and to know how true peace feel

Father god help me change my ways!

If I am to lead the next generation to a better tomorrow

I must defeat the defects of yesterday

For God doesn't sleep through happiness or sorrow

So, I can't just praise him on my best days

The youth are watching my actions and being tuned to words

Now it's a must that I teach them to not get betrayed

By the senseless things, they look up to in this crazy world

Father God help me change my ways!

I have an image to uphold when I walk in the Spirit

Don't have no time for the agony of sin

But sometimes it gets hard and my flesh doesn't want to hear it

It's a battle everyday I'm trying to win

I call on the name of Jesus to assist with His power

Because He can remove all the anger that turns to rage

That's why I pray and give Him praise every second and hour

Father God help me change my ways!

This poem is inspiration for fighting our spiritual battles. Everybody is facing the same things and we all go through similar events. We are not perfect so don't let that discourage you from your mission of going to heaven. We were made in sin and we will sin. We must fight against this sin though in order to put the devil under a footstool. I understand how we can sin without notice sometimes. It's in us my people and that's a proven fact. But God fights for us. We have to know that we are forgiven and blessed. We are god's chosen people. So ask God to help you to change your ways. You can start now by making Him your Lord and savior.

A NOBODY IS SOMEBODY

Jeremiah 29:11 For I know the plans I have for you," declares the Lord, "plans to prosper you and not to harm you, plans to give you hope and a future.

Paul persecuted Christians to the highest degree

If you followed Christ you were put to death

Until God took his sight and he heard Him speak

"You must not continue the violent threats"

See the truth is truth and it states mere facts

We are at war but we are favored, highly

If you need a reference go to The Book Of Acts

Even a nobody is somebody!

Take the story of David with a sling and rock

When he slew the great warrior Goliath

It showcases how the underdog gets to the top

When the opposition sits powerful and mighty

See the outer appearance mirages gifts and strengths

You must discern what is there inside them

In Samuel 17 a true message was sent

Even a nobody is somebody!

Then there's Adam and Eve eating the forbidden fruit

After being deceived by the baffling serpent

Which God planned Himself to fulfill the truth

So Jesus can come to serve His purpose

No matter how great or less you may think of people

Just remember that they belong to The Almighty

Check the verses and chapters to research this sequel

Even a nobody is somebody!

This was written to remind you of the individuals you may look over sometimes. Remember they are people too. They are somebody. Everyone goes through something to make them into a better person. So when a person is down and out don't neglect their needs. That person will get his chance to become great one day. Remember even a nobody is somebody!

YOUR ONLY SON THAN BECAME A MAN

1 Corinthians 14:20 Brothers, do not be children in your thinking. Be infants in evil, but in your thinking be mature.

Dear Momma I wrote you this letter

To inform you of my condition

Through all the times we spent together

I wish that I would have listened

You taught me to be a man

And to put away childish ways

But I stuck to my own plans

Not paying attention to the wisdom you gave

So now I'm honored to let it be known

That I finally have understanding

Your little boy has honestly grown

Your only son than became a man!

Woman I thank you for what you did

By making our lives seem so hard

And for taking care of three bad kids

Raising them with the Word of God

Never again will I act as a fool

And embarrass our family's name

Or try to be down by acting cool

And fall victim to this heartless game

So today I'm giving you credit

For doing the best that you can

Your #1 and I'll never forget it

Your only son than became a man!

I wrote this on how much I love and respect my mother for raising us right. Especially how she raised my two sisters. Even though when I got older I went astray but eventually a person will come back to righteousness. This woman showed us what having unconditional love for each other was by her actions and encounters with us. When our dad past away she stepped up even more because she knew children need a manly presence in their upbringing so she included my uncles and male friends of the family for aid to us. This woman is a blessing and Cheryl Ann Zardies, we love you so much. I finally can tell you that Your only son than became a man. The man God willed him to be.

THE GROUND IS NO PLACE FOR A CHAMP

Proverbs 24:10 If you falter in a time of trouble, how small is your strength.

When life throw it's best punches which might suddenly connect

And it seems you are punch drunk on the canvas

Go into a defensive mode, bob and weave to protect

All your glory and confidence to get answers

You have the power in you to excel in any effort

Take you a deep breath and mentally revamp

If you fall get up to fight it's just the force from a zephyr

The ground is no place for a champ!

When adversity and it's combos are heavily favored

And it doesn't appear that you can go pound for pound

Remember there's beauty in the struggle though the times were wavered

Because there's a strength in you that's firm and astound

Make sure to train for the bouts that won't give you a chance

Because this will earn you the title of being stamped

Being a warrior against opposition, keep your fighter's stance

The ground is no place for a champ!

Down goes Frazier, dust off and try again

For you cannot show the presence of a glass jaw

You must possess courage and hope, the recipe to win

Sometimes you may lose the battle but not the war

So when you are against all odds with problems and tests

Have the will to stay positive and be amp

Love yourself enough to go forward giving your best

The ground is no place for a champ!

This is encouragement for going through the trials and tribulations of life. Everything has it's time and season so be prepared for the good and the bad, the happy times and sad and going through joy and pain. Never give up because we all are true champions. If life sucker punches you and it might even daze you, just remember when you fall down get back up because the ground is no place for a champ like you. The new heavyweight champion of the world is you!

REAL OR FAKE

1 Samuel 16:7 But the lord said to Samuel, "Do not look upon his appearance or on the height of his stature, because I have rejected him. For the Lord sees not as man sees: man looks on the outward appearance, but the Lord looks on the heart."

If it's one thing that I've learned in this crazy world

Is that I can't be nobody but me

And through all the commotion and turmoil

Who I am is who I will be

Can't take on a role of who I'm not

Because that's not who I can see

Can't act as others want me to rock

For I wouldn't stand out as being unique

So be cautious in the choices you make

And roll with the punches on being you

Because being who you are is being true

This determines if you are real or fake!

Won't let no man thoughts decide my fate

Especially when one's thinking is petty

For I'll spend years in love before a second of hate

And this won't change for a realm or setting

This is I, me, solo, the one

Who has conquered the task of growing older

As for my identity; seed, water and sun

God gives the hardest battles to the strongest soldiers

So it is what it is when you just be sincere

And be careful with the steps you take

For what's not understood will eventually bring fear

And will expose if you are real or fake!

I wrote this on how much I love to be me and the feelings of confidence and motivation I enjoy from being proud of being myself. I once to participated in acting as a person who I knew I wasn't and wearing a real life mask. Hiding who I honestly was from others because I felt the need to play this fake role. Not understanding how everybody really loved the real me. I had to come to the realization of what lifestyle God needed me to live for my purpose and I choose His will. So in order for me to be real I had to manifest the real person inside of me who I was hiding and I love this person. This is my identity so love me or love me not because I'm going to be me. This determines if you are real or fake!

NOW I'M STONG ENOUGH TO FACE THE MADNEESS

Philippians 4:13 I can do all this through him who gives me strength.

I sat stressed out, full of grief and worried too much

Over my life's current situations

I kept my head down and my tail was tucked

Giving rule to all adversity that I was facing

See my life was a wretch until I called out for God

Who gave me many blessings that removed my sadness

He stood me up on my feet and took away my sobs

Now I'm strong enough to face the madness!

I hit rock bottom and was labeled sorry and bad

My family didn't want me around

Done some things throughout the city that I wish I hadn't

Every day I walked on enemy grounds

But when the Lord gave me vision this opened my eyes

No more blindness or living like I was a savage

I let go and let God without questioning Him why

Now I'm strong enough to face the madness!

I was bound in chains by the evilest of demons

Sometimes I thought I'll never be free

My dreams were nightmares of a million and one reasons

Of why I couldn't awake from being spiritually sleep

Oh but great is He that's within me

He's supernatural and His existence is above average

I can do all things through Jesus, I do believe

Now I'm strong enough to face the madness!

This was a time in my life where I was totally lost. Some of my family members had given up on me because of my behaviors. I spent some time homeless on the wicked streets of New Orleans. I just existed without a purpose and I would do things that made others want to hurt me. But today I am forgiven and God gave me a choice to become a new creature when I accepted Him as Lord and Savior. People God will make your worst enemy become your best friend. He can make a nobody become a somebody. You are reading the testimony of a living witness. There's no limit on what He'll do for us. Thank You Lord for Your awakening of me.

FATHER

Malachi 1:6 A son honors his father and a servant his master.

You raised me to become a man of strength

That will combine with gifts to make me whole

And you taught that through struggling I'll have to ascend

Providing the essence to my soul

You stressed hard to me about doing good in school

Saying that I should praise having an education

And to never become a follower or fool

Always displaying your dedication

You worked with me on pursuing my goals

Making sure that you paved a way

For my path in life to feature some roads

That I can travel and be okay

Your love was a blessing from the unseen

That flowed abundantly in the Spiritual form

Which caused me to stay conscience and serene

Supernaturally overshadowing the norm

You nurtured me with direction and patience

Allowing my confidence to manifest

That's why I imitated you in all my relations

Proving how we have passed the test

We exhibited the value of a mutual bond

This was designed to carry us farther

While being deeper than the roots of mankind

Is the responsibility of a father!

Dedicated to Melvin "Butchie" Zardies Jr. and to the time we shared together as father and son. I respect you so much for being a real father. Not once did you lead me astray with negativity, selfishness or misguidance. Your discipline still reins through my character today, showcasing the love, respect and leadership you instilled in me. I influence other souls to do right like you taught me. Thank you so much for your traits being exhibited through me. You'll always be the 5 Star General in my book because of the purple heart you possessed that was full of heavenly courage. I salute you for being a father because dad is just a title. Being a father is a responsibility.

SHIFT OF ATMOSPHERE

Isaiah 43:19 See, I am doing a new thing! Now it springs up; do you not perceive it? I am making a way in the wilderness and streams in the wasteland.

When you are down and out harboring feelings of despair

And no one seems to have any answers

One must channel their worries into love because nothing can compare

To get rid of the aggravation from prance

If the pressures of life are like the bursting of pipes

And the heat in the kitchen melts one's sphere

Counteract those feelings with a difference in type

You need a shift of atmosphere!

Turn negative into positive and bad into good

With just a dive into the sea of emotions

There's a treasure to discover you can find it if you could

When you open up to its magical potion

It's like abracadabra and hocus-pocus, vamoose

You can make the bad feelings totally disappear

Choose to stay happy in life in whatever you do

You need a shift of atmosphere!

Don't let a bad attitude take away your glory

Because people will turn against your credibility

Try harder to find the way of joy in your story

And you'll reach the awesome state of humility

Sweet freedom resides at the end of the rainbow

With a pot of gold to erase all your fears

Never harbor in doubt let your confidence glow

With a shift of atmosphere!

This was wrote as conformation on changing negative energies into positive. We have it in us to counteract bad or wrong thoughts with thinking about the good thoughts. This process gives you a healthy mind to think with and it makes you feel better too. So make a shift in the atmosphere when someone says bad things to you, when someone harms you and when the devil tries his tactics of making you feel bad about yourself. Channel the negative energy into some positive. You can enjoy life better and remove negative people and situations out of your life.

TIRED OF THE TEMPORARY FOREVERS

Corinthians 11:14 And no wonder, for even Satan disguises himself as an angel of light.

You get promised the world and you trust in their manipulation

Because your self-esteem and ego is considered to be low

At the slightest touch you keep falling into temptation

It's like the scent of them makes you glow

Well here's some constructive advice that should awake you from sleep

Their false paradise claims are not coming; no never

Though you won't admit it, you are wounded, cut deep

Stop falling for temporary forever's!

They put yeast on situations to make them look healthy

But in reality you're a satisfaction of the moment

They'll buy you the finest of gifts for their status is wealthy

Do you just settle because this person can do it?

Pull yourself together, momma didn't raise no fool

You know she taught you that you can do better

Stop falling victim to persuasion and follow the number one rule

And get tired of the temporary forever's!

They'll even tell you that they love you to keep you around

People will continue to use God's Word in vain

Their undermining your thoughts, like you'll are on common ground

Knowing that you are withholding sorrow and pain

Wake up from this spell, these evil spirits are traps

And call on God for help to pull it together

I guarantee you'll move forward from the misery of mishaps

Stop falling for the temporary forever's!

This is dedicated to the person who has been used or betrayed in a relationship. We are living in some evil times and some people don't care much about others feelings. They don't mind lying to you about how much they love you and if you don't have the spirit of discernment you will not be able to detect these impostors. They'll promise you the world and include god in that world so you have to be careful of who you let in your heart. Learn from every encounter with a person whether that be a male or female. Get tired of being promised those temporary forever's. Take hold of your life and be ready and on guard for these negative people. No more temporary forevers!

SOMETIMES YOU HAVE TO FAIL TO SUCCEED

Psalm 73:26 My flesh and my heart may fail, but God is the strength of my heart and my portion forever.

Keep trying because they'll be road blocks

That may delay your destination

And blind alleys could be the pit stop

To remove you from hesitation

Your goals and dreams may look to far

For you to be able to achieve

But just keep on pursuing to reap the rewards

Of accomplishing the things you believe

So when you are against all odds and hopeless

Waiting on the blessing God wants you to receive

Keep the faith and don't act off emotions

Because sometimes you have to fail to succeed!

Though having a fortune may seem off limit

And gaining peace is like chasing the wind

It could be these low stages that you've entered

That determines if your success begins

Don't get caught up in pity and shame

As if you've been folded when it's just a bend

Remember if there's no pain there's no gain

Dust yourself off and try again

So don't count yourself out when you approach hard times

For the best in you is there to retrieve

What's in the depth of you heart or the abyss of your mind

Sometimes you have to fail to succeed!

This is motivation in going through failure in life. We must understand that failure is a part of the plan to be successful. Every individual who has made it in life has a story about failing but never giving up. Keep pursuing your dreams and goals even if you fail a couple of times. This procedure builds character and shows how strong you are. So shoot for the stars people and remember sometimes you have to fail in order to succeed. Let the best come out of you and stop holding back.

CHAPTER 2: MENTAL POETRY

UNDERSTANDING OF LIFE

Proverbs 3:5 Trust in the Lord with all your heart, and do not lean on your own understanding.

When you've walked through the muddy waters

Only to still spot dry land

And you've been on the front line in Satan's army

Being guided by him hand and hand

You've been through joy and pain and sunshine and rain

Went from the bottom to the top and then back down again

But without the good times and bad

And without the darkness turning into light

You would have never grabbed a hold of

The understanding of life!

Maybe you've hit rock bottom or have sat on top of the world

And it feels like you are still searching for peace

Experienced the effects of love and hate from others and self

But managed to smile through it all and stand free

Maybe you've been blessed by angels or even cursed by demons

And you've felt as if there was not a beginning

You've prayed to God for forgiveness for the wrongs you've done

Only to get off of your knees and remain sinning

Some people live long enough finding the conclusion to know

That leaning on your own understanding brings strife

And that obedience to God's instructions is wisdom to all

When they gain the understanding of life!

Life is about ups and downs! One must rise and then he must fall. This is all a part of God's plan to mold you into the person He willed you to be. I'm a firm believer in that; "One must go through something to get somewhere." I say this because trials build character, strength, endurance, and most of all, a better you. I believe that through every negative situation, a positive outcome will reveal itself. We as people must depend on the gifts of patience, perseverance, and common sense to wait on what god is doing for us. You can't live life at a high speed because that's when accidents happen. Slow down and cruise through the road that God has constructed for you. The road to success!

GOD GIVES THE HARDEST BATTLES TO THE STRONGEST SOLDIERS

Phillippians 4:13 I can do all things through him who strengthens me.

I came, I saw, and I conquered the test

Of being my worst enemy

Never again will I seek for, nothing more or less

For I was blind but now can see

As I fought for identity my soul was doomed

And my heart was left with overwhelming doubt

There was nowhere to run, that's what I once assumed

And fighting myself was a hell of a bout

So I encourage all people to never give up

In the challenge of maturing and growing older

For in the war with the flesh enough is enough

God gives the hardest battles to the strongest soldiers!

No more will I bow to worship any idol

Or give my attention to any false god

For after struggling with self-it's all about spiritual survival

I've accepted Jesus Christ as my Lord

Now I can lead others to salvation and not wrath

So, they can be free from the chains of a carnal mind

For what a man thinks is what he attracts

And his actions will follow or coincide

So for internal affairs I suggest we dig deep

To the depths of the heart to reach Jehovah

Seeking for joy, patience, happiness and peace

God gives the hardest battles to the strongest soldiers!

One of the hardest battles we fight today is against self. If one doesn't truly possess a love for self they become their worst enemy. This state produces low self-esteem, bad character and a negative attitude toward life period. You become stuck on self and look upon self as god. In other words you worship self and become an idol. God becomes nonexistent and you neglect being conscious of His presence. But you must press on in order to overcome this sickness or possession is what I call it. Have intense battles for your identity of being a soldier of Christ. Never give up because sometimes you don't understand in life until you get deeper into your situation. Fight against the sin that's within you. You'll always have God on your side. God gives the hardest battles to the strongest soldiers! You have the power within to win.

PARADIGM SHIFT

Romans 12:2 Do not be conformed to this world, but be transformed by the renewal of your mind, that by testing you may discern what is the will of God, what is good and acceptable and perfect.

If you are stuck doing the usual or same ole same

There comes a time to change the way that you think

If you are of the adult age limit and still playing childish games

Enter new waters for that ship will sink

Evaluate your thinking and you'll know if it's right or wrong

And get the chance to give the mind an uplift

Stop being down to please others who's singing that same song

Get equipped with a paradigm shift!

See what's considered real these days is actually fake in real life

Because they are beliefs based on unsupported myths

If it's not the whole truth then it's facts are standing on thin ice

So train your mind to be conscious of this

Some think that doing wrong is so important that it overrules their decisions

Not believing in that a negative focus will make a man drift

But there is an action that one can take to change their vision

Get equipped with a paradigm shift!

Set your mind on the things above and not on this earth

And I guarantee you'll become a different breed

Leave negative people behind and shy away from all dirt

Being absent minded is a sickness of this disease

Please family renew your minds with what God has to offer

Because He is coming for His people, very swift

Or be stuck in a state of being caught up, a scoffer

Get equipped with a paradigm shift!

My people, we must let go and let God change the way we think in order to have a paradigm shift. There is some work one must put in for this to happen though. First of all you must be willing. Having an open mind serves as the foundation to this process. Secondly one must possess discipline. Discipline is having common sense to know you need correction. And most of all one must have a sincere relationship with God because staying God conscious is the answer to it all. You must become the change you want to see in the world. So become of God!

INVASION OF THE LOST KIND

Jeremiah 50:6 "My people hath been lost sheep: their shepherds have caused them to go astray, they have turned them away on the mountains: they have gone from mountain to hill, they have forgotten their resting place."

We're in a time and age that reflects what is written

Please pay attention to the signs and stay aware

Some people don't notice that they are included in a mission

Of the evil and dark forces that are here

Today's message is clear, we need to wake up out of this spell

Or become stuck in having a one track mind

Seek the Scriptures for proof, choose heaven or hell

Save your soul from the invasion of the lost kind!

Think of how people won't accept when they've done wrong to others

But when they are hurt, there's the speck in others eyes

The world is self-centered and hateful there's no love for our brothers

The only time family are together is when one dies

There's a fallen angel that's here who attacks at will

And his main focus is to devour, kill and blind

The one's who can't see past the flesh, just reacting off how they feel

Save your soul from the invasion of the lost kind!

Father I pray for our awakening because closed minds won't eat

Of the fruit that makes us full in Your Spirit

They'll stay in tune with this world, unconscious of being free

Your voice is here but some still don't hear it

There's division between the things you put here for Your reasons

We act as if You are so hard to find

In due time it will all end, don't be guilty of treason

Save your soul from the invasion of the lost kind!

Prepare your mind for the invasion of the lost kind. These are the individuals that let evil control them and they bring bad energy around everyone else. It's not them who is actually committing these acts, it's the devil using them. So, we must pray for them and uplift them because some aren't aware of this spell or possession. This state makes one feel as if they don't care about nothing. A false sense of courage is what I call it. Don't be blinded by these dark forms of bad attitudes, characters, actions and demeanors. Fight for your lives against the invasion of the lost. They're here!!!!!!

STOP BELIEVING IN MENTAL MYTHS

2 Corinthians 14: That does not surprise us, because Satan changes himself to look like an angel of light.

No wonder there's so much misery and strife

Because of some people being caught in a maze

There always focused on others instead of their lives

Letting the devil dictate all their ways

See Satan has a way to manipulate one's mind

Making them confide in what actually doesn't exist

Having them thinking of someone as a different kind

Stop believing in mental myths!

Don't keep blaming someone else for your psychological drifts

Falsifying others appearance with a mirage

Labeling them with bad names to downgrade their gifts

You are some of the most miserable people alive

Just because your mind sends a thought doesn't mean for to act

Because this trait shows that you are not fully equipped

For Satan is cunning realize how he attacks

Stop believing in mental myths!

Myths make you assume that others are always against you

When no one may be giving, you thought

While controlling your actions to a point it shows in what you do

And you speak satire about the people you heart

Even though these symptoms may be shades of indirect

And diagnostics show one could be suffering within

Studies identify these individuals of having no self- respect

They can't stop believing in mental myths!

We must be on guard against the bad seeds Satan plant in our minds. These thoughts sometimes can lead us into destruction if we act out on them. Satan is cunning, manipulative and baffling. He attack our thought process with every bad and pitiful thought that crosses our mind. His most powerful weapon is getting us to believe he's doesn't exist. I pray my brothers and sisters wake up from the sleep of allowing Satan to mentally discourage them from choosing the right path. We must always remember that he has no authority against God. We rebuke you Satan in the name of Jesus! Amen!

WHAT YOUR FEEDING THE MIND

Titus 1:15 To the pure, all things are pure, but to the defiled and unbelieving, nothing is pure; but both their minds and their consciences are defiled.

There are unseen forces that's in a battle for your soul

You better protect yourself with the armor of God

Some are good, others are evil, in search of mind control

And the aftermath is being lost and abroad

It's your company, what you think and the topic of conversation

That makes a man show his worth or what defines

Time brings change all it takes is dedication

Pay attention to what your feeding the mind!

Some of us don't notice the center of our attention

By being caught up in what's going on in the world

But there's God and then the devil giving us interventions

So the gateway to our thoughts can unfurl

Make sure you are prepared for a war is at hand

Because decisions will keep one in line

Pray for knowledge and wisdom because some won't understand

Pay attention to what your feeding the mind!

There's the law of attraction that make energy connect

It's as simple as attitudes and behaviors

And it's your choices that give rule to how you appear and reflect

So make sure you represent Our Savior

Keep your head in the game staying God conscience and aware

Because this is the time for us to elevate and shine

It's one thing for certain, God will always be there

Pay attention to what your feeding the mind!

We have a gateway to our soul that determines what you let in and out your mind and heart. This passage includes what one think, hear, see and feel. We all must focus on this area to be a better person. It dictates how your day goes, how you feel about others and self and how others look at you. The key to winning this battle is staying conscience of God. Free your mind from the filth and garbage of this world and let God give you a new way of thinking. Be careful of what your feeding the mind. Eat of the Spirit and good thoughts and actions will prevail. Have a appetite for God. Feed Up!

WHY DO YOU THINK YOU CAN THINK?

Philippians 4:8 Finally, brethren, whatever is true, whatever is honorable, whatever is right, whatever is pure, whatever is lovely, whatever is of good repute, if there is any excellence and if anything, worthy of praise, dwell on these things.

Evaluate your mental, does it all add up

Or are you one who's caught up in this world

For some people are so lost that their minds are stuck

On the ignorance and distractions that occur

Let's thank God for His wisdom because when you know, you do better

And you won't engage in being a part of the missing link

For if you are a person who just talk, without actions of a trendsetter

Why do you think you can think?

If you use your mind for negativity instead of a positive focus

You need to perform a self-inventory

If your thinking's not up to par being petty and hopeless

Try giving less attention to others and their stories

It's crazy how we can indirectly be committed to nonsense

And ignore giving our lives a sync

If you agree give your opinion, after the following comment

Why do you think you can think?

So, for future references, be mindful of your thoughts

Start counteracting the bad ones with the good

Because it's bigger than us and we're involved in a war

What I'm explaining is already understood

Whether you consciously or sub consciously deal with this issue

You have to change before your spiritual eye blink

And awake from sleep walking because society will disc you

Why do you think you can think?

My people we have to stay conscience of what's really going on around us. We are fighting battles daily, whether it be mentally, physically, emotionally or spiritually. But the battle of the mind is an important figure in becoming a better person. You have to train your mind to process and think good things. This will entitle you to better decisions and outcomes in situations. Especially in fighting the flesh. Take control of your thoughts again and shame the devil because that's the only negative presence that manipulate us into bad choices. He'll have you wondering if you can think at all. Why do you think you can think? Answer the question with truth! For me because I'm God conscience now and He win battles daily in my mind. All praise be to God! Amen!

THIS IS TELEKINESIS

Romans 7:15 I don't understand myself, for I want to do what is right, but I don't do it. Instead, I do what I hate.

Are you one who let others dictate your thoughts and moves

Having weak strategies causes an instant checkmate

Being a pond in this world is guarantee to loose

For every step is calculated, make no mistake

They are dark forces in this world with the power of possession

And some of them even spoke the name of Jesus

They say everything in life is a blessing or a lesson

Understand this is telekinesis!

There are people with authority who don't mean us well

They make the laws to control our actions

And their sole purpose is to make our lives a living hell

With all the poverty and homelessness that's happening

We have to focus and be mindful of their secrets and crafts

To be divided and conquered tore us to pieces

They don't see no race, research the proven facts

Understand this is telekinesis!

Then they are some with the craftiness of manipulation and slickness

You better be able to discern someone's motive

Always preying on nonthinkers taking advantage of their sickness

The backstabbers and snakes you have to notice

So if you know what I'm saying is on the right path

And you continue to see the evil in this species

Keep fighting for your mind because we're under attack

Understand this is telekinesis!

Notice how Satan is using others to make you react to them in bad ways or choices. This is a tactic he uses to get to us. He uses other people who sometimes don't know they are being used. And believe it or not, some know they are being used. This is Telekinesis! When something or someone dictates your thoughts or actions because of their thoughts making you react in a certain manner. And who else would be behind all the misery and strife, no one but Satan himself. Know that he's there my people so you can fight for your sprit. Don't keep falling victim to telekinesis of the serpent. There's Power in the mighty name of Jesus. Call upon His name; Jesus!

A TRADITION OF FORWARD THINKING

Genesis 19:26 But Lot's wife, behind him, looked back, and she became a pillar of salt.

Stop settling for the ignorance that's swallowing us alive

Let's take the first step to be a better person

Don't think of the natural, there's no limit, fly high

For the status of feeble minds will worsen

Be a thinker who's thinking goes above and beyond

Because it will stop your ship when it's sinking

Education is the key to opening your mind

To a tradition of forward thinking!

Let by gone be by gone, don't keep struggling with the past

Counteract those negative thoughts some that's good

Take the time out to meditate on a positive path

It's in you and you knew that you could

When discouraging thoughts come lurking , shut down what they offer

And grab hold to the mind and of what linking

Stay in tune with yourself to become a better partner

With a tradition of forward thinking!

Think ahead and beyond the average situation

Being two steps in front is your position

Train your mind to be conscience, there's no chance to be waiting

For your actions to finally hear and start to listen

Don't get held back from what God has in store

And get left behind with a thought process that's steadily shrinking

Show yourself who's in control and how you really want more

With a tradition of forward thinking!

I wrote this to encourage people to think ahead of whatever you encounter. Think it through thoroughly and make sure you include god intentions. Be positive and God will appear in every situation. I'm a firm believer in this. Make thinking forward a tradition of righteousness and being obedient to God's will. Remember my people, a mind is a terrible thing to waste. Think with a tradition of forward thinking.

EAGLES SOAR HIGH AND ABOVE

2 Samuel 1:23 "Saul and Jonathan, beloved and pleasant in their life, And in their death were not parted; They were swifter than eagles, They were stronger than lions.

There's a difference between people that separates the best from the rest

It's when one spread the wings of success to fly higher

They are not on the ground with others stirring around In mess

Their main focus is on dreams and what they desire

They have a gift when it comes to vision seeing the bigger picture

And they don't settle for less or any subs

If you are among this kind then you understand how they differ

Eagles soar high and above!

When they battle a snake it takes them out of their element

By using a switch of the atmosphere

Snakes are dominant on the ground being exceptional or celebrant

But in the air they are off balance and filled with fear

These individuals possess the powers that be

Can you feel the adrenaline pumping through your blood

The great part about this theory is that it's in you and in me

Eagles soar high and above!

They are smarter than average being reluctant to fail

In any test or situation they give great effort

When the odds are against them it's a must they prevail

Being swift with understanding and very clever

They treat tasks like it's prey, they attack until it's done

And all the secret codes to prosperity, they've debugged

Never second in competition their aim is number one

Eagles soar high and above!

This is for the individuals who soar like eagles to conquer goals, tasks and dreams. Nothing will stop them from completing what they started. Their ambition to succeed is equal to the hunt of the eagle for prey. They have confidence and a desire to bring the best out in every situation. They are some intelligent people who know it but won't boast about it with words. They let their actions speak. So don't be normal, be a eagle and soar high and above expectations. Eagles soar high and above.

CHAPTER 3: EMOTIONAL POETRY

A WOMAN'S WORTH

Ephesians 5:25 For husbands, this means love your wives, just as Christ loved the church. He gave up his life for her...

If it was one thing that I've learned from me straying away

Is to respect what she stands for in my jaunt to convey

How much she means to me and the love in my heart

She provides sight to my vision and illuminates the dark

My days are never lonely because she's on my heart and mind

Her existence sub serves purpose confirming my decision to lionize

How God delivered me a gift from being faithful when I pray

That dropped straight down from heaven and became my soulmate

It was instant gratification when her pleasure for me survived

Because through all the pain and endurance a hidden treasure arrived

From the depths of adversity and the flames of despair

My head is above water and the smoke has cleared the air

So from all the trials and failures that she continued to forgive

Not only do she get my heart I gave her my rib

For now I understand a woman's esoteric way to convert

My faith and belief in her when I discovered what she's worth

This was written on how a person goes through changes and overcomes the flaw of being selfish. When you meet that person who you feel that you'll spend the rest of your life with, that change manifests itself automatically. All praise to God first for giving you the knowledge and resources to seek change, but unconditional love for a person aids in this process too. In order to experience this love, we must love like Christ. Through Him all things are possible. Let's love with the love of Christ for this is true love. Love you guys!

WHAT IS LOVE?

1 John 4:16-18 God is love. Whoever lives in love lives in God, and God in them. This is how love is made complete among us so that we will have confidence on the day of judgment. In this world, we are like Jesus. There is no fear in love. But perfect love drives out fear, because fear must do with punishment. The one who fears is not made perfect in love.

Love is the combination of two pure hearts

In a mutual agreement to care

Love is peace and love is war

But most of all true love is rare

Love is that cool breeze on the hottest day of summer

Feeling like a blessing sent from above

It strikes the heart like lightning and make it sound like thunder

The definition of "What is Love"

Love is the fruit of the Holy Spirit

That helps us grow in times of adversity

Love is that sound of the trumpets we are waiting to hear

Which shows God's grace also His mercy

When you love make sure it's with the love of Christ

And not with just the physicality of kisses and hugs

See life is love and love is life

The definition of "What is Love"

Love is a verb it's expressed through action

That corresponds with being said in words

Love is the best form of satisfaction

Whether being delivered when seen or heard

So when I say that I love you it's comes from deep within

On the tabernacle my sacrificial offering is doves

Whether it's for an enemy, neighbor, family, or friend

The definition of "What is Love"

What do you want from love? For love can inspire us with taming the flesh. This method of love actually brings us closer to God. To live life is love and to live in love is life. Take in consideration what God gives us out of love. We should be able to give that same love in return to others. But unfortunately, this standard of love, cannot be met by some hearts in today's society. If we shall overcome the defects of unloving hearts, one must ask the Creator for a love of self. This is a genuine love that oust all fears and manifests a inner calmness, which aids in a pursuance of peace. Now think of the love we share today and ask yourself; "Could this be Love!"

I WANT YOU IN MY WORLD

Hebrews 13:4 Let marriage be held in honor among all, and let the marriage bed be undefiled, for God will judge the sexually immoral and adulterous.

The first time I locked eyes with you

Our pupils dilated as hearts

As we looked deeper into each other's soul

We saw a love that would never depart

What was seen instantly amazed us

By the care we possessed inside

All we needed was God and each other

With the same feelings that coincided

For it's an art to being fully committed

That shines better than diamonds and pearls

Let's join together in a relationship

Because I want you in my world

Though I can't touch you physically

I can feel you in my spirit

After all our unseen encounters

I can visualize your appearance

You are elegant and classy

Attracting me with the force of a magnet

With the characteristics of a masterpiece

That belongs in a beauty pageant

Though I often daydream and imagine

Of my Mrs. to be girl

I'll wait patiently for your presence

For I want you in my world

These thoughts of you regulate my heart

While they reign in the depths of my mind

Your visits to me emotionally

Bring tingling chills down my spine

Your energy keeps me level

When my feelings are off balance

Even though you are not visible

Our dealings present some challenges

That changes my state into comfort

From these moments of adjure

Stay forever being my woman

Because I want you in my world

This was written to my queen to be while incarcerated. I was waiting patiently for God to bless me with a woman that He sent to me. I prayed daily for her coming. I knew through God's presence we would shower each other with unconditional love. He sent my best female friend back into my life, who I am still with today. My soon to be wife. I feel her visits to my mind, heart, and soul were divine. For I had no idea who I was writing about in this poem. This energy still resides in what we share today. Thank you Tanya Marie Paul, for bringing out the best in me. Also for being my Mrs. to be girl, the best thing besides God that happened to me.

YOU'RE A BLESSING IN DISGUISE

Jeremiah 17:7-8 "But be blessed is the one who trusts in the Lord, whose confidence is in him. They will be like a tree planted by the water that sends out its roots by the stream. It does not fear when heat comes; its leaves are always green. It has no worries in a year of drought and never fails to bear fruit."

Woman I want to thank you for the beauty within you possess

And for making me feel a heavenly presence

By you being on my side to endure life's test

It helped me learn from my mistakes and lessons

You are my angel of protection with wings of cover

This is one of my main reasons for why

I'll lay my life down for my best friend and lover

You're a blessing in disguise

When I hear your voice it sounds like sweet hymns

Making my heart jump with joy and praise

And your touch heals my sickness, shouting out amen

You are the holy ghost when I kneel to pray

See your supernatural love never goes unseen

Trust me, my eyes are open wide

You are the message that was sent through my visions and dreams

You're a blessing in disguise

I've read through your chapters and meditated on your verses

To fully comprehend your book of life

While you gave me your grace and aided me through curses

That's why God sent you as my wife

So I've given you my faith, belief, and hope

And every day I look up in the sky

Always boasting in your favor for everyone to know

You're a blessing in disguise

When God sends that special person in your life, you'll feel His presence through it all. Everything that God touches is good and righteous, so when your significant other arrives, it'll be a good thing. Don't think that there won't be arguments and disagreements, but you'll will know each other so well that no matter what there will be perseverance. A bond that is formed with strength, trustworthiness, and loyalty. I pray for us all to have this blessing in disguise to walk the earth with us. For when you encounter their divine moments and relations, it's a guarantee you'll know.

LIFE WITHOUT YOUR MUSIC

Ephesians 5:19 Addressing one another in psalms and hymns and spiritual songs, singing and making melody to the Lord with your heart.

They'll be no more rhythmic tunes of your love and care

Which had my heart dancing to your affection

All the notes you played were seen clearly in mid air

And your melodies were to the point of perfection

You wrote a song of love with your beautiful smile

I honestly heard it, do you need me to prove it

The way you blew the horn of respect was effective and loud

Living life without your music

Since you've been gone my heartbeat plays blues

When it use to jam bombastic vibes

Your legacy continues to reign cause through love people move

And your anthem makes others comply

Your voice was a choir of angels to ears of humanity

Being an icon so it hurt us to lose it

Your sound waves of hope kept us all with sanity

Living life without your music

Your presence was a hip hop sense of wish that remains

We felt your lyrics deep down in our souls

Your character sold millions through joy and pain

And your hit records climbed the charts of being untold

So I nominate your being for the highest award

It's was a fact you were an amazing producer

Can you get an encore and a round of applause?

Living life without your music

I wrote this poem off the love I have for writing poetry. I have a deep passionate love for poetry that makes me write daily. It reminds me of the positive things I must do, of discipline, and most of unconditional love. I write for my correction and to assist others in becoming a better person. Iron sharpens iron, so we need each other to grow. It goes hand and hand.

OH, HOW I LOVE TO FEEL BEING FELT

John 13:8 Peter said to Him, "Never shall You wash my feet!" Jesus answered him, "If I do not wash you, you have no part with Me."

I can feel how you feel the overwhelming power

When your heart is in total control

Because being felt is the water to nurtured flowers

And the essence to light up one's soul

So if feelings can lead to the right decisions and choices

I'll continue praying for good spirit and health

And let the angels sing hymns in their heavenly voices

Oh how I love to feel being felt

It's those feelings inside or the thoughts of your mind

When God answers your visions and dreams

It's a wonderful feeling with Him on your side

For in war we need Christ on our team

Now if you feel how I feel give Him glory and praise

Through life or death and when your crying out for help

For I was lost and He guided me out life's maze

Oh how I love to feel being felt

I can feel the marriage between me and the Savior

I said the phrases of, "I surrender" and "I do"

Because He loved me even through my worst behavior

Leading my steps when I took one He took two

So if you believe in that feeling of the Holy Ghost

You have more than the worlds riches and wealth

Be a fisher of man when you set sail of your boat

Oh how I love to feel being felt

God created us with the mind and heart. Two of the most powerful organs on the human body. It's common sense to me that He gave us these gifts for a reason. We partake in divine communication with God through our thoughts and feelings. One has to honestly pay attention to this theory. You are aware when you do something right or wrong from either a thought or feeling after you take action. This within itself concludes that God is speaking to us. We must assure that we obey him at all times because it's our responsibility. This is encouragement to listen people. Listen to the whispers of your mind and heart that tells you to make the right decisions. This displays loyalty and a highly favored reverence for Him. I love feeling His presence and I understand that in obedience, prayer, and meditation that I'm honoring His Name. Oh how I love to feel being felt! He feels my unconditional love for Him through my heart and mind.

I MISS THAT TEENAGE LOVE

Proverbs 17:17 A friend loves at all times, and a brother is born for a time of adversity.

I'll never forget our times together

Or all the priceless moments we've shared

Even though those memories will last forever

My heart still shows that care

Though we both were young and didn't quite understand

What was behind our kisses and hugs

I'll always reach out to for hand and hand

Because I miss that teenage love

I think of the times when only you had the answers

To what my hardest test was asking

And how you walked the school halls strutting and prancing

While you wore my letterman jacket

How you cheered for me when I scored points in games

Made me shoot for your touches and rubs

Though the years have passed and things are not the same

I miss that teenage love

From the dances, to prom night, and on to graduation

How did the time move so fast

Now it's on to the big campus for orientation

I thought that young love would always last

If there's a way to rekindle those flames

That made our what it once was

I'm hoping not to wait in vain

Because I miss that teenage love

Love is everlasting. Even when one has ended a relationship with someone does not mean you have to stop loving them. The devil needs us to hate people. He feeds of negative energy for power. We as godly individuals must understand that he has no power against God and counteract his evil tactics with righteousness. Let's stay winning with love. We have no reason or purpose to hate anyone. Even when someone has wronged you, love will over power their sin. I love you all and I can honestly say this today because there was once a time when I could not. Live in love and love and live!

I'M SITTING ON TOP OF THE WORLD

1 John 3:16 This is how we know what love is: Jesus Christ laid down his life for us. And we ought to lay down our lives for our brothers and sisters.

Out of all life's valuable experiences

Discovering love sits as the best

It's moments of happiness and healthy feelings

Makes our chances of hatred lessen

By being never ending and truly sincere

It's an emotion that one should prefer

And by being of the Sprit it oust all fears

Love I'm sitting on top of the world

I don't have bow down on a certain level

When man does not act as he should

Because it's clear that his actions are of the devil

There's a vibe that he's up to no good

When you know where you stand against evil temptation

Then you sit fully developed as being mature

Choose The Way to resist these traps of Satan

Joy I'm sitting on top of the world

Though I believe and I have not seen

My Savior look me face to face

He's appears in my visions, also in dreams

Next to Our Father in His heavenly place

Then His miracles, blessings, healings, and Mind

Confirms how my soul is preserved

He's not always there when I call, but always on time

Faith I'm sitting on top of the world

Believe in what God can do for you and you can be sitting on top of the world too, literally. The trials we face here are only test that we are highly favored to past if we sincerely accept Jesus as Lord. We are more than conquerors people. Through Christ anything is possible, so why can't we choose to live in peace. We don't have to live in turmoil and entertain the evil of this world. We are getting closer and closer to his coming my brothers and sister. So let's prepare ourselves by sitting on top of the world. Know that you can defeat evil with good. We rebuke you Satan in the Mighty Name of Jesus!

SHE HAS ME SITTING ON A THRONE OF GOLD

Genesis 2:22 And the rib that the Lord God had taken from the man he made into a woman and brought her to man.

Her love gives off the power of a king

It's reigns in my heart and mind

She's like chariots of fire journeying to bring

Sweet freedom to all mankind

She governs my emotions being just and fair

That she queenly takes care of my soul

Her kingdom of love makes my feelings declare

She has me sitting on a throne of gold

Her enchanting demeanor eases my consolation

As if I've sown my faith on cloud nine

While her majestic style of presentation

Reaps the reward of beautiful sunshine

She castles my heart with joy and charm

To a point that she makes me whole

And my love for her makes royalty form

She has me sitting on a throne of gold

I desire her riches of compassion and peace

Like a knight on the quest for the grail

She pays much homage for my actions are meek

And in return I offer her my hail

So I've been crowned and abundantly blessed

With a queen to live happy and grow old

Through trials, adversity, tribulation, and test

She has me sitting on a throne of gold

We all have that special person whose love makes you feel like king or queen. They've served their purpose of having a royal love with you by honoring the heavenly commandment of love. They know how to treat you, what to tell you in times of spiritual battles, their love serves you with passion. Well this is encouragement to treat them the same. Show them that powerful love of the king or queen that you are and sit them on a throne of gold. Pull the Excalibur from their heart and rule with love, peace, and understanding. You'll have chants of, "Hail to the king or queen" for loving them with and live happily ever after.

NOTHING LIKE THAT MOTHERLY LOVE

Luke 1: 46-48 And Mary said: "My soul glorifies the Lord and my spirit rejoices in God my Savior, for he has been mindful of the humble state of his servant. From now on all generations will call me blessed,

While I was in your womb, I could hear your voice

As you spoke to me with compassionate words

And I listened to your heartbeat which gave me a choice

To accept a life with your discipline conferred

I know people do love me and that's without no doubt

But you survived birthing me, my first hug

That's why I sincerely cried once you pushed me out

Because there's nothing like that motherly love

When my dad left the earth it was your will and push

That drove me to do the best I can

You kept me focus on education, I made good grades in the books

And made sure I understood what it was to be a man

There was no limit or extent you would not go for me

I'm so happy for sharing your blood

That's why it was necessary to cherish all your care that be

Because there's nothing like that motherly love

And still today there's no change in how you got my back

Your support of me puts tears in my eyes

That's why I'll never disrespect you with immature acts

Because I know someday I'll time will expire

This is from me to you expressing the things that's unsaid

You showed me what true love really was

Dear Mother, thanks for your realness to raise me in those days

Because there's nothing like that motherly love

We only get one mother from birth that we share the same blood with. I'm not insinuating that a motherly presence can't manifest herself in someone's life. If that be the then this person deserves praise as well. But I'm reflecting on the love a mother has for her child or children. They'll go beyond normal circumstances to supply the needs to their children. Unfortunately, some people will never understand because they show this through their ungodly actions. We must keep praying for them. So to all, honor your father and mother because God commanded us to do so. Show them the unconditional love of God.

CHAPTER 4: SPIRITUAL POETRY

The Chosen Don't Stop We Keep Going

1 Peter 2:9 But you are his chosen people, the King priests. You are a holy nation, people who belong to God. He chose you to tell about the wonderful things he has done. He brought you out of the darkness of sin into his wonderful light.

When God has a calling on your life and a purpose.

That doesn't mean things are going to be perfect.

They'll be temptations and trials, that's a part of the devil's circus.

It's to make you discouraged and worried.

But through it all stand bold, holding the faith of a mustard seed.

Because you'll need it on the battlefield, you'll just know it.

Keep doing the work of The Lord, showing your love through good deeds.

The Chosen don't stop we keep going!

They'll be some days when you possess a strong faith like Job

and at other times you'll have the anger of Cain.

He gives us strength like Samson, even when Delilah's are posed.

As if they are for us but come to bring us pain.

We are Peter and Paul to His church until the finish

and through Christ's Love we will keep on soaring.

But most of all we are gods because we are made in His image.

The Chosen don't stop we keep going!

We endure adversity as if we have the spirit of Joseph

and we persevere like The Mother of God.

We trust in the secrets of war because we know we're Christ's soldiers,

for the road will be narrow and not broad.

We lean not on our understanding because of a passion for Wisdom,

and the miracles, favor, and blessings keep flowing.

The knowledge of knowing Him gives us a supernatural vision,

because the Chosen don't stop we keep going!

Being chosen by God comes with responsibility. We as a people must recognize that we've been appointed to perform supernatural duties. Let's all pray today for the courage, strength, and patience to understand the tasks we have at hand. Though times may get rough and it may seem as if the odds are against you, just remember; The Chosen Don't Stop We Keep Going!

Dance like David did!

2 Samuel 6:12-15 12: Later people told David, "THE Lord has blessed the family of Obed Edom and everything he owns, because God's Holy Box is there." So David went and brought God's Holy Box from Obed Edom's house. David was very happy and excited. 13: When the men who carried the Lord's, Holy Box had walked six steps, they stopped and David sacrificed a bull and a fat calf. 14: David was dancing in front of the lord. He was wearing a linen ephod. 15: David and all the Israelites were excited- they shouted and blew the trumpet as they brought the Lord's Holy Box into the city.

Oh, what a wonderful feeling to experience His presence

After being stuck in a mental prison

And then He spoke to me about life's lessons and blessings

Also about how His son is Risen

Now I can't see no bars and I'm free of the chains

Because I'm withholding the faith of a little kid

I can hear the music of the Spirit, when I call out His name

So I can dance like David did!

When I'm in those same streets there's no worry or fear

Because my lord covers me with protection

I can feel as we move, being confident that He's near

Celebrating to His songs of progression

My spirit hops, skips, and spins when He defeats the acts of Satan

And one can see this from the way that I live

No more partying with the devil in the masquerade of hatred

Now I can dance like David did!

It's how I escaped the flames from the fiery pit

When I was lost and possessed by evil demons

I craved desires of the flesh, had no purpose, just existed

Living life with no direction or meaning

But now things have changed in my heart and mind

And to look at me as the same man I do forbid

For I am a new creature in Christ, being one of a kind

Now I can dance like David did!

We all experience the ups and downs of our Spiritual battle against the accuser. Sometimes it may seem as if God is letting you fight alone. Trust in how much He trust in your ability to overcome Satan with the powers that be inside us. Oh you of little faith! Matthew 8:26. God is in the midst of every situation, circumstance, and outcome of every fight. We must believe that being made in His image gives us an advantage over the evil forces of the world. Keep fighting my brothers and sisters, so we can dance like David did to the tunes of feeling God's presence through it all.

Samson and Delilah

Judges 16:10 Then Delilah said to Samson, "You have made a fool of me; you lied to me. Come now, tell me how you can be tied."

Just like Samson, we were chosen before birth for God's work

And time after time we fail at His missions

We let obstacles and adversity become Delilah's of hurt

Or we let the Philistines subtract multiple choices from our additions

God gave us the same strength to tear down life's columns

And to defeat the questions of evil desires

Don't let Satan cut your hair because obedience speaks volumes

This is the story of Samson and Delilah!

We kill young lions every day in the form of temptation

And come right back and eat honey from the unclean

With the jawbone of a donkey we can take down what we're facing

We have to be sure that we're playing for God's team

Sometimes we're blind to the fact like our eyes were poked out

But our Spiritual eyes see straight through all the mirages

God is with us for protection we must believe without doubt

This is the story of Samson and Delilah!

We must obey God's calling with a respect and reverence

And not go against the grain like tied up foxes

Through God's grace we have the power to eat of Bread that's unleavened

And travel with the Shepard who knows His flock is

The predecessors of peace, prosperity, and triumph

That's why we press on and we wait on God's timing

To win the race of all races for in the marathon we run

This is the story of Samson and Delilah!

My people we must pay close attention to the tactics and effort of evil. Watch the actions of individuals and listen to what comes out of their mouth. God gave us the Spirit of discernment to identify when things aren't right. Pray for all because some are possessed with bad spirits and don't even know it. They live by the means of this world and that's all what matters, trying any and everything to do the work of the devil. But remember God says resist the devil and he will flee. James 4:7. There's power in The Mighty Name of Jesus.

David has Killed Tens of Thousands!

1 Samuel 18:7 The women sang, "Saul has killed his thousands, but David has killed tens of thousands."

How could a king be so jealous of his soldier at war

Let this be a reminder modern Saul's still today

When others chant for your victory make sure it's from the heart

Because the beast is on the hunt to kill and slay

They're thinking you want their kingdom being a sign of the weak

Envy is full, especially if there's riches and power

But with God on your side, you'll continue to be meek

David has killed tens of thousands!

Saul saw that God had left him to comfort and mold David

Pay attention to one of the seven deadly sins

When the people were for David, Saul didn't like what they did

He set up a plan for David's demise to have him end

See the moral of the story is to monitor each other's flesh

For it's like a hungry king of the jungle on the prowl

The Spirit is always there through all temptations and tests

David has killed tens of thousands!

Some people are so self-centered because their hearts are corrupt

They see your David characteristics and they'll attack

Though we all kings we must become servants and trust

That the Father will supply us with what we lack

We are blessed with gifts in many forms and different ways

So, let's believe in His footsteps that we are following

For He's coming, we're living in the last days

David has killed tens of thousands!

Jealously is a form of hatred that leads many people to sin. We must monitor of flesh because it invites itself into situations sometimes. People we must stay God conscience daily so that we may fight against the darkness of this world. God supplies us with the secrets of war, so we may defeat the acts of Satan. Pray that God protects your mind from the cunning and baffling spells of the devil. God bless you all and pray, pray, and pray more.

Jesus turns water into wine!

John 2: 9-10 They did so, and the master of the banquet tasted the water that had been turned into wine. He did not realize where it had come from, though the servants who had drawn the water knew. Then he called the bridegroom aside and said, "Everyone brings out the choice wine first and then the cheaper wine after the guests have had too much to drink; but you have saved the best till now."

Do what He tells you, was the Message through talking

Did you catch a woman preaching The Word

There were six large water pots used in ceremonial washings

The number of incompletion had to be heard

He needed the leaders to see because they would not believe

So He showed them completion, right before their eyes

All this was written, so our faith can be conceived

Jesus turns water into wine!

Water represents life and wine is the Blood of our Savior

Let's pay attention to the chapters and verses

We need to part from worldly ways and change our behaviors

By opening up to gifts and negating the curses

It's as simple as the Lord speaking Knowledge and Wisdom

Illuminating where the doesn't shine

Oh how I love how His prophecies come in dreams and visions

Jesus turns water into wine!

In his teachings, lifestyle, who He chose as disciples

That convinces me that He walked in the flesh

How He gives us Spiritual weapons to fight against our rival

And gives us Scriptures to assist through tests

So I thank God for his blessings and the lessons He teach

For without Him there's no renewal of the mind

Through the glory and power, His Word I'll preach

Jesus turns water into wine!

We must understand the power in God's Word, especially when we speak it. As believers we can speak things into existence by having faith and belief in what we pray for. Family, God spoke a clear message in this passage. It was that we must obey and trust in what He reveals to us. Keep praying that your gateways to the soul may open. Remember, Jesus can turn water into wine and with that being said let Him do the same in your life.

If your listening God Speaks

2 Timothy 3:16 All scripture is breathed out by God and profitable for teaching, for reproof, for correction, and for training in righteousness,

The word communicate is a connection between persons or places

Whether being silent or through things that may be heard

Well there's one form that's consistent with life's Spiritual basics

It's the message that comes from God's Word

God talks to us through Scripture and Spirit

If you sow to comprehend then it's what you'll reap

He's in there in midst, pause, can you hear Him?

If your listening, God speaks!

He's in the heart and mind battling for your soul

Better pay attention to the sharpening sound

It's the iron clashing with evil, from His double edged sword

To keep our feet upon some solid ground

Though His words aren't heard like they would be from man

He still is The Father of freedom of speech

Giving you correction and discipline high above the laws of the land

If your listening, God speaks

He talks through the fresh breath of air when you awake in the morning

And the one on one prayer at night

Or when you meditate deeply and intimacy is forming

Also through conviction when your wrong or right

So stay in tune with His voice for it is everlasting salvation

Whether it comes in English, Arabic, or Greek

Because when we miss what He says it breaks down our foundation

If your listening, God speaks!

We must learn to listen to God as He communicates to us. We often miss out on His lessons and blessings by ignoring God's voice. Let's open our minds and hearts to a divine relationship with Him so we can be in tune with His messages. God speaks to us daily, whether it be through prayer, meditation, or communion. Brothers and sisters we must be wise enough to listen!

Death couldn't destroy Him!

Acts 1:3 To these He also presented Himself alive after His suffering, by many convincing proofs, appearing to them over a period of forty days and speaking of things concerning the kingdom of God.

Hollowed be thy name, thy kingdom come

Sweet baby Jesus our Savior

The Alpha and Omega, thy will be done

Thank you Lord for showing so much favor

The Messiah, Lamb of God you take away the sins of the world

They know not what they do so forgive them

King of Kings, Lord of Lords through the insults they hurled

Even death couldn't destroy Him!

Heavenly Father, Our Rock, there's power in Your Name

You were faithful until the very end

With a crown of thorns on You and for Your garments, played games

And You still carried our crosses, what a great Friend

What a great act of propitiation, that is what I call love

I can imagine the pain from limb to limb

And they still till this day, drag Your name through the mud

Even death couldn't destroy Him!

He that come to You must believe that You are

They try to make us think Your psychological control

But we must diligently seek Him for the wrath of Spiritual war

And for the sake of fighting to save our souls

If I was on that hill, I would have asked for Your forgiveness

Just like one of the men who did then

So, for all who don't believe, you'll better make it your business

Even death couldn't destroy Him!

Don't let death destroy things in your life, whether it be physical, mental, emotional, or spiritual. Keep pushing through it all because God is assisting in every situation. Keep living life and try hard to conquer your dreams and goals. So, whenever adversity steps in your path to kill your dreams, remember that even death couldn't destroy Him!

You are perfect, full of love!

Luke 6:35 But love your enemies, do good to them, and lend to them without expecting to get anything back. Then your reward will be great, and you will be children of the Highest, because he is kind to the ungrateful and wicked.

There's not a day that goes by when I don't sense You're there

Even through the hard times You offer assistance

It's a blessing just to breathe, a fresh breath of air

And to be a part of Your wonderful existence

I'd like to thank You for being made in Your image

I give You glory and praise just because

And for the instructions to live righteous, in Your Book it is written

You are perfect, full of love!

I thank You for peace, for Your calmness and serenity

Also Your Knowledge, Wisdom, and Understanding

Through Your Grace, I get a burst of supernatural energy

Which is awesome or perhaps outstanding

My alone time with You simply makes me better

I'll spend a life time wrapped in Your hugs

Ain't nothing like prayer, just me and You together

You are perfect, full of love!

That's why I sing Hallelujah to worship Your name

Making me dance like David did

Concentrated on One God, destiny, One Destiny, with One Aim

With the faith of a little kid

Your Psalms and Proverbs offer me immediate comfort

It's a blessing to be covered by Your Blood

The fathom of Your Word means understanding Biblical Numbers

You are perfect, full of love!

Make sure you are rooted in the greatest commandment of all. Jesus gave His life for us, so we should love one another with the same love. If we believe in this love it'll help in every area of your life. There's nothing like God's love because He's perfect.

My Final Destination!

Revelation 14:13 Then I heard a voice from heaven say, "Write this: Blessed are the dead who die in the Lord from now on." "Yes," says the Spirit, "they will rest from their labor, for their deeds will follow them."

When my last day come, I won't feel no sorrow

Because I've planned for the Promise Land

See my spirit will ascend for my body was borrowed

Amen, some people just won't understand

They'll sing amazing grace, how sweet the sound

But I'll be partaking in divine liberation

I once was lost, but now I'm found

This is my final destination!

When the hour of conformation finally arrives at my temple

I won't be afraid to walk into the Light

Because I'm confident I'll get in, no matter what they say I've been through

No more deaths, just everlasting life

What my God has to offer motivates my quest to my quest to the pearly

gates

And to be exact I was tired of waiting

With belief, hope, and a mustard seed of faith

This is my final destination!

I'll pray for our forgiveness after I give Him praise

Giving thanks for His mercy and love

Because being in the flesh needed some supernatural aid

You were there every step for us

No more earthly distractions from thinking with a carnal mind

This is my day to arise, His Revelations

I went back to the dust and everything will be fine

This my final destination!

My people, we all must face an end that's coming. For most people, they don't want to acknowledge the thought of this fact, but one day it'll call. I'm not trying to scare anyone, I'm giving you the blue-print to knowing how to deal with death. Pray for comfort and God will lead you to victory. It's all about getting prepared for your final destination!

Construction of me being renewed!

Romans 12:2 And do not be conformed to this world, but be transformed by the renewing of your mind, so that you may prove what the will of god is, that which is good and acceptable and perfect.

God I'm grateful for the people You instilled in my life

For they have truly become part of me

Also for the family and friends Who's constructive insight

Showed me the things I could not see

So, I want to take this opportunity to express my heart

To a part of me that made me whole and true

And show gratitude to the ones who played their parts

In the construction of me being renewed!

Now my foundation is built upon a Solid Rock

He covers me through my slips and falls

I'm a new creature through Him from being a part of His flock

Even when my back is against the wall

Lord I thank You for the strength, you've imbedded in my life

Cause now my temple can withstand the blues

I appreciate Your presence whether it being day or night

In the construction of me being renewed!

I'm built with honor, respect, and Spiritual strength

Along with integrity, perseverance, and serenity

I'm storm proof now, so I'll withstand high winds

Now I can pass fiery temptations of the enemy

There's nothing better than being rooted in the Word of God

Because it builds character and saves you; from you

For He's our Lord that gives protection with thy staff and thy rod

In the construction of me being renewed!

This is encouragement for anyone who is in the rebuilding process in their lives. Maybe you've been through a lot and experienced some down time. This is to uplift you. God puts people in your circle for His sole purpose and reason. He gives you a foundation to build yourself around. They are there to mold you into the person you were born to be. Keep these support systems around you and I guarantee they'll be a sky rise being built in you. Seek the Scriptures for help and let God renew your mind.

THE CONCLUSSION

First and foremost, I would like to give thanks to my Lord and Savior for giving me the courage to tell my story through poetry. This is my testimony to show what God can do. Through my experience in life He kept me covered in His arms of protection. I've encountered many let downs and betrayals that lead me to not trusting anyone but when I surrendered my life to God, this changed my mindset and heart. I feel these stories are forms of motivation and inspiration to others and can lead others to be better. I understand how my writings help me and others so I will continue to let God use me. I'm so thankful for what God has done for me and I will continue to honor and praise His name. I've grown into the person that God put me here to be. I understand my purpose now and I will deliver His message to my fellow beings daily.

Secondly, I would like to thank a friend indeed that I reached out to for guidance and od lead me the right way. He has inspired me to write and to believe in myself again no matter what I encountered in my past. He helped me believe in me again. Though we don't talk on the phone or see each other daily, when we do meet it's nothing but positive conversations. I appreciate this guy so much, Thanks Mr. Myles Berrio, for letting God use you as a vessel. Can't wait to see what our next adventure is.

I also would like to thank my soon to be wife who showed me a better side of life by exposing me to God's way of unconditional love. She has my back to the fullest and I can't deny loving her the same in return. All my life I was searching for the love she has for me. Thank you, Tanya, for always bringing out the best in me. My experiences with you help me write love poems on a whole different level. You make me better!

Then there's my family, friends, life experiences, doubters and supporters. I appreciate everything that help me change my life. I could not have done it without you all and the events that took place. I believe everything happens for its sole purpose and reason. A special thanks goes out to my mother Mrs. Cheryl Zardies, who stood by my side through it all. The real definition of a mother. My experiences with her helped me write a lot of what I went through. Thank you so much. I want to thank my sisters Tamara Zardies and Kierra Oxley. These women possess the love my mother and fiancée have for me, being a godly love. Then there's the late Melvin Zardies Sr. and Jr., two men that help me become a man. Without these two godly presences in my life there was no way I would have made it through the storm. They live forever through me and my family. To all the positive role models in my life both deceased and alive, I appreciate you all dearly. Thanks for the tough love and guidance and for sticking with me no matter what. To my best friends Clarence (Jerome) Rhyans, Adam (Chew) Shelmire, Clarence (Big Clay) LaCour, Damon (Dee) Stokes, Norvelle Williams and Jermale Ayers, all I can say is "Wow!" Words can't explain the love I have for you guys. Our times together taught me some valuable lessons, especially when I went astray. There are none like you guys, it's a shame I had to learn that the hard way. And to every other person who had a positive effect in my life, whether friend or family, I sincerely appreciate you all. You too are a part of my story. You know who you are.

Also I would love to thank my uncle Tyrone (T-Bird) Brooks for his special partaking in me becoming the man I am today. Since day one of my dad being deceased he was there for me, teaching and molding me into the person who could withstand the storms of life that will come. I've always looked up to him, even still today. I discerned traits in him that I quickly knew were needed to survive in life. Though some of the things I learned from him were considered street smarts, I want to thank him so much for being real with me and exposing me to the things that being ignorant to can bring one to their demise. I use a lot of his saying and teachings still today. Salute! Family Ties For Life! O.T.F. (Only The Family)

And last to all I've been through both the good and bad because this with The Lord on my side helped me to become the man I am today. This is my story through poems. My truth will inspire someone to change and help them to stray away from negativity. If I can do it anyone can because I was stuck at the point of no return and returned. When God is for you, who can be against you. So to my reader, keep your head held high in battling temptation because you can win. Keep your faith strong when facing adversity because this too shall pass. You are more than a conqueror through Christ and you will prevail in tests and trials. I encourage you to tell your story and start living in a Poetic Spirit. I love ya'll and be blessed.

Made in the USA
Middletown, DE
24 December 2022